THE POWER OF POSITIVE RELATIONSHIPS

RELATIONSHIP

SOMDEV YADAV

Contents

Contents

ONE

DEFINITION OF POSITIVE RELATIONSHIPS

Positive relationships are connections between individuals that are characterized by mutual respect, trust, kindness, and a shared sense of well-being. These relationships provide a source of support, encouragement, and happiness and can greatly enhance our quality of life.

B. Importance of Positive Relationships in Our Lives

Emotional Support

Positive relationships provide emotional support, a sense of belonging, and the comfort of knowing that someone is there for you in good times and bad. This emotional support can be especially important during difficult times, such as the loss of a loved one, relationship problems, or financial stress.

Increased Happiness and Satisfaction

Positive relationships also have the power to increase happiness and overall life satisfaction. Studies have shown that people with strong social connections are more likely to report higher levels of happiness and a greater sense of purpose in life.

Improved Physical Health

In addition to the emotional benefits, positive relationships can also have a positive impact on our physical health. Research has found that people with strong social networks are less likely to experience chronic conditions, such as heart disease and depression, compared to those with weaker social networks.

C. The Different Forms of Positive Relationships

Positive relationships can take many different forms, including romantic relationships, friendships, family relationships, and professional relationships. Each type of relationship can bring its own unique benefits and challenges, but all positive relationships share common traits, such as mutual respect, trust, and open communication.

II. The Challenges of Building Positive Relationships

A. The Importance of Building Positive Relationships

While positive relationships can bring many benefits, they can also be challenging to build and maintain. Negative relationships, such as toxic friendships or unhealthy romantic partnerships, can drain our energy and bring us down, while positive relationships can lift us up and provide a source of support and encouragement.

B. Overcoming Obstacles to Building Positive Relationships

There are many obstacles that can stand in the way of building positive relationships, including trust issues, communication problems, and a lack of empathy. However, by learning effective communication skills, practicing empathy, and building trust, it is possible to overcome these challenges and build positive relationships that enhance our lives.

III. Conclusion

A. Summary

Positive relationships play a critical role in our lives, providing emotional support, increasing happiness and life satisfaction, and improving physical health. Whether in the form of romantic relationships, friendships, family relationships, or professional relationships, positive relationships can bring many benefits, but they can also be challenging to build and maintain.

B. Final Thoughts

Building positive relationships is an ongoing process, but the effort is well worth it. By learning effective communication skills, practicing empathy, and building trust, we can overcome the challenges of building positive relationships and create meaningful connections that enhance our lives and bring us joy.

TWO

Definition of Positive Relationships

Positive relationships are those that bring us joy, fulfillment, and a sense of well-being. These relationships are characterized by mutual respect, trust, kindness, and open communication, and they play a critical role in our lives.

B. Why Positive Relationships are Important

Positive relationships bring many benefits to our lives, including emotional support, increased happiness and life satisfaction, and improved physical health. These relationships also provide us with a sense of belonging and help us to feel connected to others, which can be especially important in times of need.

C. The Different Forms of Positive Relationships

Positive relationships can take many different forms, including romantic relationships, friendships, family relationships, and professional relationships. Each type of relationship brings its own unique benefits and challenges, but all positive relationships share common traits, such as mutual respect, trust, and open communication.

II. The Benefits of Positive Relationships

A. Emotional Support

Positive relationships provide us with emotional support, a sense of belonging, and the comfort of knowing that someone is there for us in good times and bad. This emotional support can be especially important during difficult times, such as the loss of a loved one, relationship problems, or financial stress.

B. Increased Happiness and Life Satisfaction

Positive relationships have the power to increase happiness and overall life satisfaction. Studies have shown that people with strong social connections are more likely to report higher levels of happiness and a greater sense of purpose in life.

C. Improved Physical Health

In addition to the emotional benefits, positive relationships can also have a positive impact on our physical health. Research has found that people with strong social networks are less likely to experience chronic conditions, such as heart disease and depression, compared to those with weaker social networks.

III. The Importance of Positive Relationships in Childhood

A. Building Positive Relationships in Childhood

Positive relationships are important to develop from an early age. Childhood is a critical time for building social connections and learning the skills needed to form and maintain positive relationships in adulthood.

B. The Long-Term Benefits of Positive Relationships in Childhood

Research has shown that positive relationships in childhood can have a lasting impact on our lives, including better mental and physical health, increased life satisfaction, and stronger social networks in adulthood.

IV. Conclusion

A. Summary

Positive relationships are a critical part of our lives, providing emotional support, increased happiness and life satisfaction, and improved physical health. Whether in the form of romantic relationships, friendships, family relationships, or professional relationships, positive relationships play an important role in our well-being and bring many benefits to our lives.

B. Final Thoughts

The importance of positive relationships cannot be overstated. By making an effort to build and maintain positive relationships, we can create meaningful connections that bring us joy, fulfillment, and a sense of well-being. These relationships are essential for our emotional, mental, and physical health, and they can help us to lead happier, more fulfilling lives.

THREE

Building Positive Relationships

The Importance of Building Positive Relationships

Building positive relationships is a critical part of our lives, as these relationships bring us joy, fulfillment, and a sense of well-being. Positive relationships are characterized by mutual respect, trust, kindness, and open communication, and they play a critical role in our happiness and overall well-being.

B. Why Building Positive Relationships Can be Challenging

While building positive relationships can bring many benefits, it can also be challenging. Life can be busy and stressful, and it can be difficult to make time for relationships. Additionally, some people may struggle with social anxiety, communication difficulties, or other challenges that can make building relationships difficult.

C. The Benefits of Overcoming these Challenges

Despite the challenges, overcoming them and building positive relationships is worth the effort. Positive relationships can bring many benefits to our lives, including emotional support, increased happiness and life satisfaction, and improved physical health.

II. Steps for Building Positive Relationships

A. Start by Building Self-Confidence

Building positive relationships begins with building self-confidence. By working on self-care and self-confidence, we can become more confident in our interactions with others, which can help us to build positive relationships.

B. Be Open and Honest

Open and honest communication is key to building positive relationships. By being open and honest with others, we build trust and establish a foundation for mutual respect.

C. Practice Active Listening

Active listening is an important skill for building positive relationships. By taking the time to truly listen to others, we can show that we value their thoughts and feelings, which can help to build mutual respect and trust.

D. Show Kindness and Compassion

Kindness and compassion are critical components of positive relationships. By showing kindness and compassion to others, we can help to build trust, respect, and open communication, which are all key components of positive relationships.

E. Make Time for Relationships

Building positive relationships takes time and effort. By making time for relationships, we can strengthen our connections with others, which can help to bring greater happiness and fulfillment to our lives.

III. Building Positive Relationships in Different Contexts

A. Romantic Relationships

Building positive romantic relationships requires effort, communication, and a commitment to mutual respect and trust. By working on these skills, we can build strong and fulfilling romantic relationships.

B. Friendships

Building positive friendships requires effort and time, but the rewards can be significant. By making time for our friends, being open and honest with them, and showing kindness and compassion, we can build strong and meaningful friendships.

C. Family Relationships

Building positive family relationships can be especially challenging, but the rewards can also be especially great. By working on communication skills, showing kindness and compassion, and making time for family, we can build strong and supportive family relationships.

D. Professional Relationships

Building positive professional relationships is critical for success in the workplace. By being professional, showing respect, and being open to feedback and collaboration, we can build positive professional relationships that can lead to greater success and fulfillment in our careers.

IV. Conclusion

A. Summary

Building positive relationships is a critical part of our lives, bringing joy, fulfillment, and a sense of well-being. Despite the challenges, overcoming them and building positive relationships is worth the effort, as these relationships can bring many benefits to our lives, including emotional support, increased happiness and life satisfaction, and improved physical health.

FOUR

COMMUNICATION IN POSITIVE RELATIONSHIPS

The Importance of Communication in Relationships

Communication is a critical component of positive relationships, as it helps to build trust, respect, and understanding between individuals. Good communication skills are essential for resolving conflicts, expressing needs and wants, and building strong and supportive relationships.

B. Common Communication Barriers in Relationships

Despite the importance of communication in relationships, many people struggle with communication. Common communication barriers in relationships include misunderstandings, miscommunication, and emotional barriers, such as fear, anger, and anxiety.

C. The Benefits of Overcoming Communication Barriers

Overcoming communication barriers can bring many benefits to relationships, including increased trust, greater understanding, and improved conflict resolution skills.

II. Communication Skills for Positive Relationships

A. Active Listening

Active listening is a critical communication skill for positive relationships. By taking the time to truly listen to others, we can show that we value their thoughts and feelings, which can help to build mutual respect and trust.

B. Empathy

Empathy is the ability to understand and share the feelings of others. By practicing empathy, we can build greater understanding and compassion in our relationships, which can lead to stronger and more supportive relationships.

C. Assertiveness

Assertiveness is the ability to express our needs and wants in a clear and confident manner. By being assertive, we can communicate our needs and wants effectively, which can help to build mutual respect and understanding in our relationships.

D. Conflict Resolution Skills

Conflict is a natural part of any relationship, but the way we handle conflict can make a big difference in the health and happiness of our relationships. By developing effective conflict resolution skills, we can resolve conflicts in a way that is respectful and helps to build stronger relationships.

III. Improving Communication in Relationships

A. Practice Effective Communication Skills

Improving communication in relationships requires practice and effort. By actively working on our communication skills, we can improve our ability to communicate effectively, which can help to build stronger and more supportive relationships.

B. Seek Professional Help

For some individuals, communication barriers may be too difficult to overcome on their own. In these cases, seeking professional help, such as therapy or counseling, can be a valuable tool for improving communication and building stronger relationships.

C. Create a Safe Space for Communication

Creating a safe and supportive environment for communication is critical for building positive relationships. By encouraging open and honest communication, and avoiding criticism and judgment, we can create a safe space for communication that can help to build stronger and more supportive relationships.

IV. Conclusion

A. Summary

Communication is a critical component of positive relationships, and good communication skills are essential for building trust, respect, and understanding between individuals. Despite the challenges, overcoming communication barriers and improving communication skills can bring many benefits to relationships, including increased trust, greater understanding, and improved conflict resolution skills.

B. Final Thoughts

By making an effort to improve our communication skills, we can build stronger and more supportive relationships that bring us joy, fulfillment, and a sense of well-being. Whether we are working on our communication skills on our own or with the help of a professional, the effort is worth it, as effective communication is key to building positive and meaningful relationships.

FIVE

TRUST IN POSITIVE RELATIONSHIPS

The Importance of Trust in Relationships

Trust is a fundamental aspect of positive relationships, as it forms the foundation for mutual respect, understanding, and intimacy. Without trust, relationships are often fraught with anxiety, fear, and insecurity, making it difficult to build strong and supportive connections.

B. The Benefits of Trust in Relationships

When trust is present in relationships, individuals are able to build deeper and more meaningful connections. Trust helps to create a sense of security and comfort, allowing individuals to be their true selves, share their thoughts and feelings, and grow and evolve together.

C. Trust-Building Activities in Relationships

Building trust in relationships requires effort and commitment, but it can be achieved through a variety of trust-building activities. These activities can include regular communication, practicing honesty and transparency, and working together to resolve conflicts.

II. The Role of Honesty and Transparency in Trust-Building

A. The Importance of Honesty in Relationships

Honesty is a critical component of trust-building in relationships, as it helps to create a sense of security and comfort, and builds mutual respect and understanding.

B. The Benefits of Transparency in Relationships

Transparency is the practice of being open and honest about our thoughts, feelings, and actions, which can help to build trust in relationships. By being transparent, individuals can create a sense of accountability, which can strengthen trust and deepen connections.

III. Resolving Conflicts to Build Trust

A. The Impact of Conflicts on Trust

Conflicts can have a significant impact on trust in relationships, as they can create feelings of hurt, anger, and resentment. It's important to handle conflicts in a way that is respectful and helps to build trust, rather than damaging it.

B. Conflict Resolution Techniques for Building Trust

There are a variety of conflict resolution techniques that can help to build trust in relationships, including active listening, compromise, and mediation. By working together to resolve conflicts, individuals can improve their ability to communicate effectively, build mutual respect and understanding, and deepen their connection.

IV. Overcoming Trust Issues in Relationships

A. Addressing Trust Issues

When trust issues arise in relationships, it's important to address them in a respectful and open manner. This can involve having honest and open conversations, seeking professional help, and working together to rebuild trust.

B. Healing from Past Trauma

Past trauma can have a significant impact on trust in relationships, and healing from this trauma may be necessary to build trust and deeper connections. This may involve seeking professional help, such as therapy or counseling, and working through the pain and hurt to move forward.

V. Conclusion

A. Summary

Trust is a fundamental aspect of positive relationships, and is essential for building mutual respect, understanding, and intimacy. Trust can be built through a variety of activities, including regular communication, honesty and transparency, and conflict resolution. When trust issues arise, it's important to address them in a respectful and open manner, and seek support and guidance as needed.

B.Final Thoughts

Building trust in relationships takes time and effort, but the rewards are worth it. When trust is present, individuals are able to build deeper and more meaningful connections, and enjoy the benefits of strong and supportive relationships. Whether we are working to build trust in our existing relationships or striving to create new relationships, the power of trust cannot be underestimated.

SIX

EMPATHY AND COMPASSION N POSITIVE RELATIONSHIPS

Empathy and compassion are two crucial elements in building positive relationships. They are the foundation of a strong bond between individuals and are essential for creating a deep sense of connection and understanding. Empathy is the ability to understand and share the feelings of others, while compassion is the feeling of caring and concern for others. In this book, we will delve into the importance of these qualities in relationships and how they can lead to a stronger and more fulfilling connection.

Understanding Empathy and Compassion

Empathy and compassion are often used interchangeably, but they have distinct differences. Empathy is the ability to understand and experience the emotions of others. It allows us to put ourselves in someone else's shoes and feel what they are feeling. Compassion, on the other hand, is the feeling of caring and concern for others. It is the drive to help and support others in needed.

The Benefits of Empathy and Compassion in Relationships

Empathy and compassion are not just good qualities to have in life, but they also bring numerous benefits to relationships. When empathy and compassion are present, communication improves, leading to deeper understanding and reduced conflict. Relationships become stronger and more fulfilling, as individuals feel emotionally connected and valued. These benefits can lead to a more harmonious relationship, where both partners feel heard and understood.

The Science of Empathy and Compassion

The science behind empathy and compassion has been extensively studied, and research has shown that these qualities are linked to various physical and mental health benefits. People who practice empathy and compassion have lower levels of stress and anxiety, as well as better physical health outcomes. Additionally, these qualities have been shown to increase feelings of happiness and well-being in individuals.

Cultivating Empathy and Compassion in Relationships

Empathy and compassion are not traits that individuals are born with, but rather qualities that can be developed and cultivated over time. In this chapter, we will explore various ways in which individuals can build their empathy and compassion skills, such as practicing active listening, putting yourself in others' shoes, and being more present in the moment.

Overcoming Obstacles to Empathy and Compassion

While empathy and compassion are crucial elements in positive relationships, they can also be challenging to develop and maintain. In this chapter, we will discuss common obstacles that can hinder the development of empathy and compassion and provide practical strategies for overcoming these challenges. These strategies include managing negative emotions, practicing self-reflection, and seeking support from loved ones.

Conclusion:

In conclusion, empathy and compassion play a crucial role in positive relationships. By understanding these qualities, individuals can build a stronger and more fulfilling connection with their partners. Through the cultivation of empathy and compassion, individuals can enjoy improved communication, deeper understanding, and a more harmonious relationship.

SEVEN

The Benefit of Positive Relationships for Physical Health

The connection between our physical health and the relationships we have with others is undeniable. Research has shown that our relationships play a crucial role in our overall health and well-being. From reducing stress and promoting happiness to preventing chronic diseases and increasing life expectancy, positive relationships offer numerous benefits for our physical health.

The Power of Social Support:

One of the most important ways positive relationships can benefit our physical health is through social support. When we have a network of supportive friends and family members, it helps to reduce stress and depression, and in turn, can prevent chronic illnesses such as heart disease and stroke. Social support also provides a sense of belonging, which is essential for overall well-being and happiness.

Stress Reduction:

Stress is a leading cause of numerous physical health problems, including heart disease, high blood pressure, and digestive disorders. Positive relationships, especially with intimate partners, can play a vital role in reducing stress and promoting relaxation. The emotional support and intimacy that comes with a positive relationship can help to relieve stress and anxiety, allowing individuals to feel more relaxed and at peace.

Healthy Habits:

Positive relationships can also encourage healthy habits and behaviors. For example, having friends who are physically active can motivate us to be more active and healthy, leading to improved overall health. Additionally, our partners and family members can provide support and encouragement when it comes to making healthier lifestyle choices.

Preventing Chronic Diseases:

Positive relationships can also help to prevent chronic diseases by reducing the risk factors that contribute to their development. For instance, social support can help to reduce stress, which in turn can reduce the risk of developing chronic illnesses such as heart disease, stroke, and diabetes. Furthermore, having positive relationships can also help individuals maintain healthy habits, such as eating well and staying physically active, which are crucial in preventing chronic diseases.

Conclusion:

In conclusion, positive relationships are essential to our physical health and well-being. From reducing stress and promoting healthy habits to preventing chronic diseases and increasing life expectancy, the benefits of positive relationships for physical health are undeniable. By nurturing positive relationships and building a supportive network of friends, family, and intimate partners, individuals can improve their physical health and enjoy a happier, more fulfilling life.

EIGHT

BUILDING POSITIVE RELATIONSHIPS IN CHILDHOOD

The foundation of healthy relationships is laid in childhood

Positive relationships in childhood can have a lifelong impact on a person's wellbeing

The Importance of Positive Relationships in Childhood:

Positive relationships in childhood promote healthy emotional and social development

Children with positive relationships are more likely to develop resilience, confidence, and self-esteem

Positive relationships in childhood are associated with better academic performance and mental health outcomes

Building Positive Relationships in Childhood:

Building positive relationships with peers: Encouraging children to play and interact with others, teaching them social skills, and helping them navigate conflicts

Building positive relationships with adults: Providing a safe and supportive environment, modeling positive relationships, and nurturing strong bonds with family, teachers, and other caregivers

The Impact of Negative Relationships in Childhood:

Negative relationships in childhood can have a damaging impact on a child's development

Children who experience bullying, neglect, or abuse may struggle with anxiety, depression, and low self-esteem

Conclusion:

Building positive relationships in childhood is crucial for a child's overall wellbeing and future success

By providing children with supportive relationships, they will be equipped to form healthy relationships in adulthood and throughout their lives.

NINE

MAINTAINING POSITIVE RELATIONSHIPS IN ADULTHOOD H

Introduction:

Positive relationships are just as important in adulthood as they are in childhood

Maintaining positive relationships in adulthood requires effort, communication, and a commitment to growth

The Importance of Positive Relationships in Adulthood:

Positive relationships in adulthood provide a sense of belonging, support, and happiness

Good relationships with friends and family can improve mental and physical health outcomes, and increase life satisfaction

Positive relationships in the workplace can lead to job satisfaction, career advancement, and financial stability

Building and Maintaining Positive Relationships in Adulthood:

Building new relationships: Joining social groups, volunteering, and pursuing hobbies can provide opportunities to form new relationships

Maintaining existing relationships: Staying in touch, being a good listener, and being open and honest with loved ones can help to strengthen existing relationships

Overcoming conflict: Conflict is inevitable in any relationship, but it can be resolved through effective communication, compromise, and forgiveness

The Impact of Negative Relationships in Adulthood:

Negative relationships can have a significant impact on a person's wellbeing and happiness

Negative relationships can lead to stress, anxiety, and depression, and can interfere with work, family, and personal goals

Conclusion:

Positive relationships are essential for a fulfilling and happy life, and maintaining positive relationships in adulthood is key

By being proactive, communicative, and compassionate, people can build and maintain positive relationships that last a lifetime

TEN

THE IMPACT OF TECHNOLOGY ON POSITIVE RELATIONSHIPS

The impact of technology on positive relationships has been a topic of much discussion and debate in recent years. While technology has made it easier for people to connect and communicate with each other, even from great distances, excessive use of technology can also lead to decreased face-to-face communication and real-life social interaction, which can harm positive relationships.

Studies have shown that people who spend more time on their phones and social media have a lower level of satisfaction in their relationships compared to those who spend less time on technology. Additionally, excessive technology use can lead to feelings of loneliness, depression, and anxiety, which can further harm positive relationships.

However, technology can also be used in positive ways to enhance and maintain positive relationships. For example, video calls and instant messaging can help people stay connected with loved ones who live far away. Social media can also be a great way to share memories and experiences with friends and family.

In order to maximize the positive impact of technology on relationships, it is important to use technology in moderation. This means setting limits on how much time is spent on devices and making an effort to engage in face-to-face communication and real-life social interactions. By doing so, it is possible to maintain and strengthen positive relationships even in a technology-filled world.

ELEVEN

Overcoming Negative Relationships and Building Positive Ones is a crucial chapter in the book "The Power of Positive Relationships." In this chapter, we will delve into the different types of negative relationships and how they can impact our lives. We will discuss various strategies for overcoming negative relationships and transforming them into positive ones. This chapter will also provide practical tips and tools for building new and healthy relationships while maintaining the positive ones.

The first step in overcoming negative relationships is to recognize their existence and impact. Negative relationships can cause a lot of stress and anxiety, leading to emotional and mental distress. They can also have a significant impact on our physical health, leading to various health problems. It is essential to understand that negative relationships are not just limited to romantic or intimate relationships but can also include friendships, family relationships, and work relationships.

Once we have recognized the negative relationships in our lives, we can start to work on transforming them into positive ones. This can be done by improving communication skills, developing trust, and fostering empathy and compassion. Practicing self-care and setting boundaries can also help to create healthy relationships.

Technology has had a significant impact on our relationships, both positive and negative. While technology has made it easier to connect with people from all over the world, it has also led to the decline of face-to-face interaction and can contribute to feelings of loneliness and isolation. To overcome the negative impact of technology on relationships, it is important to balance our technology use and prioritize in-person interaction.

In conclusion, overcoming negative relationships and building positive ones is an essential part of cultivating a happy and fulfilling life. By following the strategies outlined in this chapter, readers will be able to create healthy and supportive relationships that will contribute to their overall well-being.

TWELVE

THE ROLE OF FORGIVENESS IN POSITIVE RELATIONSHIPS

Forgiveness is a critical aspect of positive relationships. When we hold onto resentment and anger towards someone who has hurt us, it can eat away at us and negatively impact our relationships with that person and others. On the other hand, forgiveness can bring peace and closure to a relationship, allowing us to move forward and form stronger, more positive connections with others.

In order to foster forgiveness in a positive relationship, it's important to understand the different motivations behind our actions and emotions. We may feel justified in our anger, but taking the time to reflect on why someone may have acted the way they did can help us see the situation from their perspective and find a path towards forgiveness.

Additionally, it's important to practice self-compassion and self-forgiveness. When we are able to forgive ourselves for our own mistakes and shortcomings, it becomes easier to extend that same compassion and forgiveness to others.

Finally, open and honest communication is key to fostering forgiveness in a relationship. When we can express our feelings and concerns in a non-judgmental and understanding way, it becomes easier to resolve conflicts and move towards forgiveness.

THIRTEEN

Gratitude is one of the most powerful tools for fostering positive relationships. It is the act of appreciating and acknowledging the good things in life, and it has been shown to have numerous benefits for both mental and physical health. In this chapter, we will explore the many ways in which gratitude can enhance the quality of our relationships, both with ourselves and with others.

Gratitude helps us to shift our focus from what is lacking in our lives to what is abundant. When we practice gratitude, we become more attuned to the good things in life and are more likely to appreciate the positive aspects of our relationships. This shift in perspective can have a profound impact on our happiness and well-being, as well as our relationships with others.

One of the ways in which gratitude can enhance our relationships is by increasing feelings of connection and intimacy. When we express gratitude to our loved ones, it sends the message that we value and appreciate them, and this can strengthen our bonds with them. Gratitude can also help to improve our communication skills, as it encourages us to express our feelings more openly and authentically.

Gratitude can also have a positive impact on our self-esteem and confidence. By acknowledging the good things in our lives, we are able to see ourselves in a more positive light, and this can help us to feel more confident and secure in our relationships. Furthermore, gratitude can also help to increase resilience, as it helps us to focus on the positive aspects of life even during difficult times.

In addition to its benefits for individual well-being, gratitude can also help to enhance the quality of our relationships with others. When we express gratitude, we become more supportive, compassionate, and understanding towards others. This, in turn, can foster a more positive and supportive environment, which can help to strengthen our relationships with those around us.

Finally, gratitude can help us to develop a sense of purpose and meaning in our lives. By focusing on what is good in our lives, we are more likely to feel fulfilled and content, and this can have a positive impact on all of our relationships, including those with ourselves, our family and friends, and even with our work.

In conclusion, gratitude is a powerful tool for fostering positive relationships, and it can be cultivated through intentional practices such as keeping a gratitude journal, expressing appreciation to others, and focusing on the positive aspects of life. By incorporating gratitude into our daily lives, we can enhance our well-being, improve our relationships with others, and create a more positive and fulfilling life for ourselves and those around us.

FOURTEEN

Positive relationships play a crucial role in career success. A positive working environment with supportive colleagues, a great mentor, or a helpful boss can make a big difference in one's professional life. Research has shown that employees who have strong relationships with their coworkers and supervisors tend to be more productive, engaged, and satisfied with their jobs.

Having a supportive network of colleagues can also lead to better opportunities for professional growth and career advancement. People who have positive relationships at work are often more likely to receive promotions and receive recognition for their accomplishments. In addition, people who have supportive colleagues are more likely to feel empowered to take on new challenges and responsibilities, which can further advance their careers.

Having strong relationships with supervisors can also be beneficial for one's career. A supportive boss can provide guidance, offer opportunities for professional development, and provide feedback that can help an employee grow in their career. Furthermore, a positive relationship with a boss can also help to reduce stress and increase job satisfaction.

In addition, having positive relationships with clients and customers can also play a role in career success. When individuals have positive relationships with clients and customers, they are more likely to establish trust and credibility, which can lead to more business opportunities and increased success.

In conclusion, the power of positive relationships in one's career cannot be overstated. By building and maintaining supportive relationships with coworkers, supervisors, clients, and customers, individuals can increase their professional satisfaction, productivity, and success.

FIFTEEN

In the world of personal finance, having a positive relationship can play a significant role in financial stability. A supportive partner or friend can provide emotional support during tough times, and can help hold one accountable for making smart financial decisions. On the other hand, negative relationships, such as those plagued by arguing about money or mistrust, can contribute to financial stress and instability.

It's important to approach financial planning and decision-making as a team, whether in a romantic relationship or with a close friend or family member. Having open and honest discussions about money can help prevent misunderstandings and set clear expectations for each person's role in managing finances.

In addition, having a positive relationship can also provide opportunities for joint financial planning and investment. For example, couples may decide to pool their resources to purchase a home, start a business, or save for retirement. This can lead to increased financial stability and security, as the costs and risks of these decisions are shared.

However, it's also important to be mindful of power dynamics in relationships, and to ensure that each person's autonomy and financial independence are respected. For example, one partner should not have control over all of the couple's finances or make unilateral decisions without the other partner's input.

In summary, positive relationships can provide emotional support, accountability, and opportunities for joint financial planning that contribute to financial stability. On the other hand, negative relationships can cause financial stress and undermine stability. It's important to foster open and honest communication about finances and to respect each person's autonomy and independence.

SIXTEEN

POSITIVE RELATIONSHIPS AND CONFLICT RESOLUTION

Conflict resolution is an important aspect of positive relationships as conflicts are bound to arise in any relationship, be it personal or professional. The key to resolving conflicts in a positive manner is through effective communication, empathy, and a willingness to compromise.

In positive relationships, conflicts are not seen as an obstacle, but rather as an opportunity for growth and improvement. The individuals involved in the relationship are open to finding a solution that works for both parties and do not allow their emotions to cloud their judgment. They understand that conflicts are a natural part of any relationship and work together to find a mutually acceptable solution.

Effective communication is crucial in conflict resolution. Both parties must be willing to listen to each other's perspectives and express their own needs and concerns in a respectful manner. By having open and honest communication, individuals can avoid misunderstandings and find a solution that addresses the root cause of the conflict.

Compromise is also an important aspect of conflict resolution in positive relationships. Both parties must be willing to give and take in order to reach a resolution that works for both of them. A compromise does not mean that one party wins and the other loses, but rather that both parties are willing to make sacrifices in order to maintain the relationship.

In addition, individuals in positive relationships understand the importance of empathy and putting themselves in the other person's shoes. This helps to build understanding and respect and allows both parties to come to a resolution that takes into account each other's needs and concerns.

In conclusion, conflict resolution is an integral part of maintaining positive relationships. By using effective communication, empathy, compromise, and a willingness to work together, individuals can resolve conflicts in a positive and productive manner, leading to a stronger and healthier relationship.

SEVENTEEN

THE IMPORTANCE OF SELF-CARE IN POSITIVE RELATIONSHIPS

Self-care is an essential aspect of maintaining positive relationships. When individuals prioritize their own well-being and take care of themselves, they are better equipped to build and maintain healthy relationships with others. Self-care allows individuals to recharge and rejuvenate, reducing stress and anxiety and increasing emotional stability.

Self-care can take many forms, such as regular exercise, adequate sleep, healthy eating habits, meditation, or simply taking time for hobbies and interests. By engaging in self-care activities, individuals can improve their overall mood, increase their energy levels, and boost their resilience, making them better equipped to handle the challenges and conflicts that inevitably arise in relationships.

In order to maintain positive relationships, it is essential to understand the importance of self-care and make it a priority. This means setting boundaries and making time for activities that promote well-being and personal growth. Individuals should also avoid overcommitting themselves and recognize when they need to take a break or prioritize their own needs.

Additionally, self-care should also be incorporated into relationships themselves. This can mean making time for shared self-care activities, such as exercise or couples therapy, or simply taking time to prioritize the well-being of both partners. By making self-care a central part of relationships, individuals can deepen their connections and build more resilient, positive relationships.

In conclusion, self-care is a crucial component of positive relationships. By prioritizing self-care, individuals can improve their own well-being, become better equipped to handle challenges in relationships, and build stronger, more resilient connections with others.

EIGHTEEN

The Importance of Boundaries in Positive Relationships

When it comes to relationships, setting and maintaining clear boundaries is essential for both personal growth and the health of the relationship. Boundaries are the invisible lines that separate one person from another, and they help to define each person's unique identity and personal space. When these boundaries are honored and respected, both partners can feel secure and supported.

However, when these boundaries are not respected or are crossed, it can lead to feelings of anger, resentment, and emotional pain. For this reason, it is important for individuals to learn how to set and maintain healthy boundaries within their relationships.

Here are a few tips for establishing and maintaining healthy boundaries:

Identify what your boundaries are: This is the first step in creating healthy boundaries in your relationships. Take time to reflect on what values and behaviors are most important to you and what you are not willing to tolerate.

Communicate your boundaries clearly: Once you have identified your boundaries, it is important to communicate them clearly and respectfully to your partner. This can help to prevent misunderstandings and conflicts down the line.

Be consistent: Maintaining your boundaries consistently is important in order to avoid mixed messages and confusion. When you establish a boundary, it is important to stick to it, no matter what.

Be open to compromise: While it is important to maintain your boundaries, it is also important to be open to compromise when necessary. When two people are in a relationship, it is common for their boundaries to overlap or conflict. In these situations, it is important to have open and honest communication to reach a resolution that works for both partners.

Prioritize self-care: When you are in a relationship, it can be easy to prioritize your partner's needs over your own. However, it is important to prioritize self-care and put your own needs first. This can help to maintain a healthy balance in the relationship and prevent you from feeling drained or taken advantage of.

In conclusion, the importance of boundaries in positive relationships cannot be overstated. By setting and maintaining healthy boundaries, individuals can create more fulfilling and supportive relationships with their partners, friends, and family. By prioritizing self-care and open communication, individuals can cultivate positive and healthy relationships that are built to last.

NINETEEN

The future of positive relationships is promising and holds immense potential for growth and evolution. With advancements in technology and the increasing awareness about the importance of relationships, it is expected that the future of positive relationships will be shaped by a more holistic and inclusive approach. The emphasis will be on fostering positive relationships that are built on mutual respect, trust, empathy, and understanding.

One of the major trends in the future of positive relationships is the integration of technology into relationships. With the increasing reliance on technology, it is expected that technology will play a significant role in maintaining and enhancing positive relationships. This will include virtual communication platforms, relationship management tools, and personalized relationship-building algorithms.

Another trend that is expected to shape the future of positive relationships is the increasing focus on mental health and wellness. The importance of self-care and the role that relationships play in promoting mental and emotional wellness will be emphasized. This will lead to a greater emphasis on nurturing positive relationships and managing negative ones.

The future of positive relationships will also see a greater emphasis on diversity and inclusivity. With increasing globalization and cultural exchange, it is important to recognize the unique experiences and perspectives of individuals from different backgrounds and to build positive relationships that are inclusive and respectful of differences.

In conclusion, the future of positive relationships holds immense promise and is expected to be shaped by an increased focus on technology, mental health and wellness, diversity, and inclusivity. By building and nurturing positive relationships, individuals can cultivate greater happiness, fulfillment, and well-being, both for themselves and for those around them.

TWENTY

Positive relationships can be strengthened and enhanced through learning and growth. This involves being open to new experiences and continuously improving oneself in order to become a better partner, friend, or family member. By learning and growing together, individuals can deepen their connection and create a more fulfilling relationship. This can involve taking courses or workshops, engaging in activities that challenge or stimulate both partners, or simply trying new things together.

Incorporating new experiences into the relationship can provide a sense of novelty and excitement that can help rekindle the spark in a relationship. Learning and growth can also bring partners closer by creating shared experiences and memories. Additionally, continuously developing and improving oneself can increase self-esteem, which in turn can make individuals more confident in their relationships.

However, it's important to remember that growth and learning should not just be focused on fixing one's own flaws, but also on learning new things and discovering new passions as a couple. This can create a more dynamic and exciting relationship, while also fostering a deeper sense of connection. By engaging in activities and experiences that challenge and inspire, couples can become better partners and individuals, resulting in a more positive relationship overall.

TWENTY-ONE

The Importance of Quality Time in Positive Relationships

Quality time refers to intentional, focused and undivided attention given to another person. It involves being present and engaged with the other person and making them feel valued and heard. Quality time is a critical aspect of positive relationships as it helps to strengthen the bond between two people and improve communication.

When two people spend quality time together, they create an opportunity to connect on a deeper level. They can talk, listen, and understand each other in a way that is not possible through any other means. This type of interaction allows individuals to build trust and feel more connected to each other.

Additionally, quality time can improve intimacy in relationships. When two people prioritize spending time together, it sends a message that they value and care about each other. As a result, both individuals feel more appreciated and loved, which can lead to increased intimacy and emotional connection.

Quality time does not have to be elaborate or expensive. It can be something as simple as taking a walk together, cooking a meal, or watching a movie. The key is to make sure that the focus is on the person and not on distractions such as phones or computers.

In conclusion, quality time is a crucial aspect of positive relationships. It helps to build trust, intimacy, and emotional connection. Making quality time a priority in relationships is a simple and effective way to enhance and maintain positive relationships.

TWENTY-TWO

Positive relationships have a profound impact on our interactions with others. They can foster a sense of connection, build trust, and provide a foundation for mutual support and understanding. These relationships can inspire us to be our best selves, and they can help us to develop a greater appreciation for the people around us.

When we have positive relationships, we are more likely to feel confident and secure in our interactions with others. This, in turn, can make us more open and receptive to others, and more willing to share our thoughts and feelings. As a result, we are more likely to establish deep and meaningful connections with the people around us.

Moreover, positive relationships can also have a contagious effect, as our positive attitudes and actions can influence others. This can create a cycle of positivity that can spread throughout our communities and beyond.

However, it is important to note that the impact of positive relationships on our relationships with others is not limited to the people we interact with directly. Our positive relationships can also have a ripple effect on the world around us. For example, if we are in a positive relationship with our spouse, this can positively impact our relationship with our children, our colleagues at work, and even strangers we encounter in our daily lives.

In conclusion, the impact of positive relationships on our relationships with others is undeniable. Positive relationships can help us to build stronger and more meaningful connections, foster mutual respect and understanding, and create a more positive and supportive environment for all.

TWENTY-THREE

The benefits of positive relationships in marriage and intimate relationships are numerous and can significantly improve the overall quality of life for partners. A strong, supportive relationship can provide emotional security, comfort, and stability, allowing partners to feel valued, loved, and accepted.

Positive relationships in marriage and intimate partnerships can also help partners to better cope with stress, anxiety, and life's challenges, as they can support each other during difficult times and provide a source of comfort and encouragement. Additionally, positive relationships can foster intimacy, deepen emotional connections, and improve physical health, as partners feel more relaxed, less stressed, and more content in their relationship.

Moreover, positive relationships can also play a significant role in the success and longevity of a marriage or intimate partnership. Research has shown that couples who have strong relationships and engage in positive behaviors such as communication, empathy, and affection have lower rates of divorce and are more likely to stay together over the long-term.

In conclusion, positive relationships in marriage and intimate partnerships provide partners with a foundation of love, support, and security that can help them navigate life's ups and downs, maintain healthy relationships with others, and achieve greater overall happiness and well-being.

• 53 •

TWENTY-FOUR

Positive relationships in the workplace can have a significant impact on job satisfaction, productivity, and overall success. Research has shown that employees who have positive relationships with their colleagues and supervisors are more likely to be engaged and committed to their work. They are also more likely to feel a sense of belonging, which can contribute to a more positive and supportive work environment.

Good working relationships can help to reduce stress and conflict in the workplace, as employees are more likely to collaborate and support one another when they have strong relationships. This can lead to better problem-solving, decision-making, and overall teamwork.

Additionally, having positive relationships in the workplace can lead to increased job security, as employees are more likely to recommend each other for promotions and opportunities. They are also more likely to support one another in times of need, such as during a difficult project or when facing a personal issue.

It is important for employees to actively work on building and maintaining positive relationships in the workplace. This can include taking the time to get to know one's colleagues, being open to constructive feedback, and being a good listener. It can also involve taking the initiative to help others, being positive and supportive, and being proactive in resolving conflicts when they arise.

Having positive relationships in the workplace can bring numerous benefits to both the individual employee and the organization as a whole, making it an important aspect of work life to focus on.

TWENTY-FIVE

Positive relationships between parents and children are crucial for the well-being and development of children. These relationships can have a significant impact on children's future success, happiness, and overall life satisfaction. Positive parent-child relationships are characterized by love, affection, mutual respect, open communication, and trust.

For parents, building and maintaining a positive relationship with their child can help to strengthen the bond between them, increase understanding and empathy, and foster a supportive and nurturing environment. This can in turn improve the child's self-esteem, emotional intelligence, and resilience, as well as their ability to form healthy relationships with others later in life.

For children, positive relationships with their parents can provide a sense of security and stability, as well as a foundation for their overall emotional and mental well-being. Children who have strong and positive relationships with their parents are more likely to develop a positive self-image, and feel more confident and secure in the world around them. This can help to prevent behavioral problems, substance abuse, and mental health issues in children, and contribute to their overall success in life.

It's important to note that positive relationships with parents can look different for different families and children, but the key is to find what works best for each individual situation. This may involve spending quality time together, setting clear boundaries, and actively communicating and listening to each other.

In conclusion, positive parent-child relationships are essential for children's overall well-being and success, and should be a priority for all parents. By putting in the effort to build and maintain these relationships, parents can help to ensure that their children have the best possible foundation for a happy and fulfilling life.

TWENTY-SIX

Friendships can play a significant role in our lives and can impact our overall well-being and happiness. Positive relationships with friends can bring joy, comfort, and support, especially during difficult times.

When we have positive relationships with friends, we feel comfortable being ourselves, and we can share our thoughts, feelings, and experiences without judgment. Our friends can serve as a sounding board for our ideas, and they can offer support and encouragement when we need it most.

Positive relationships with friends also provide opportunities for growth and learning. Friends can challenge us to try new things and expand our horizons. They can also provide a different perspective on situations, which can help us see things in a new light and make better decisions.

Having positive relationships with friends also has numerous benefits for our mental health. Research has shown that having a strong social support system can improve our mood and reduce feelings of stress and anxiety. It can also improve our self-esteem and boost our overall confidence.

In order to maintain positive relationships with friends, it's important to be intentional and invest time and energy into the relationship. This can involve regularly checking in with your friends, making time for quality one-on-one time, and being open and honest with each other. It's also important to be supportive and understanding when your friend is going through a difficult time, and to be a good listener when they need someone to talk to.

Overall, positive relationships with friends can bring immense joy, comfort, and support to our lives, and are an essential component of our overall well-being and happiness.

TWENTY-SEVEN

Diversity and inclusiveness are critical components of positive relationships. A diverse and inclusive environment can lead to a broader understanding of different perspectives and experiences, helping to build bridges between individuals and foster a sense of community. Inclusive relationships promote respect and understanding of others, and allow people to feel valued and appreciated, regardless of their differences.

When individuals feel included and respected in their relationships, they are more likely to contribute to the growth and well-being of the relationship. Additionally, diversity in relationships can bring a wealth of new ideas and perspectives, leading to a more dynamic and innovative environment.

However, it is important to recognize that building diverse and inclusive relationships requires effort and a willingness to understand and respect differences. This involves actively listening to and engaging with individuals from different backgrounds, being open to new perspectives, and promoting equality in all aspects of the relationship.

Moreover, it's important to acknowledge and address any biases or prejudices that may exist, and work to create a safe and inclusive environment for everyone involved.

In conclusion, diversity and inclusiveness play a crucial role in positive relationships, and by promoting these values, individuals can strengthen their connections with others and create a more harmonious and inclusive community.

TWENTY-EIGHT

Positive relationships and spirituality are often interconnected, as having positive relationships can provide a sense of comfort, support, and fulfillment, which can enhance one's spiritual beliefs and practices. On the other hand, a strong spiritual foundation can also contribute to the development and maintenance of positive relationships.

Spirituality can refer to a person's connection to a higher power, their own sense of purpose and inner wisdom, or a sense of interconnectedness with all beings. Regardless of one's specific beliefs, spirituality can provide a source of comfort and meaning in life, which can positively impact relationships.

For example, having a strong spiritual connection can help individuals to practice empathy and compassion towards others, and to approach relationships with a sense of humility and understanding. Spirituality can also encourage individuals to forgive others, and to maintain a positive outlook even in the face of challenges.

Moreover, engaging in spiritual practices with others, such as attending a place of worship or participating in meditation or prayer groups, can strengthen relationships. These shared experiences can provide a sense of belonging and foster a deeper connection between individuals.

In summary, positive relationships and spirituality can complement and enhance each other, leading to greater well-being and satisfaction in life. By fostering positive relationships and a strong spiritual foundation, individuals can create a supportive network that provides comfort, growth, and fulfillment.

TWENTY-NINE

The impact of positive relationships on community can be significant and far-reaching. Positive relationships help to foster a sense of connection and belonging among community members, which can lead to a stronger, more resilient community overall. When individuals are connected through positive relationships, they are more likely to work together to solve problems and address challenges, and they are also more likely to feel invested in their community and committed to making it a better place.

In addition, positive relationships can also help to create a more supportive environment for all members of the community. When individuals feel supported by those around them, they are more likely to have the confidence and resilience needed to overcome obstacles and pursue their goals. This can have a cascading effect, as individuals who are thriving and successful are more likely to give back to their community and help others to do the same.

At the same time, positive relationships can also help to reduce conflicts and tensions within a community. When individuals are able to communicate openly and respectfully with one another, they are less likely to experience misunderstandings or disagreements that could escalate into larger conflicts. This can lead to a more harmonious and cooperative community overall.

In short, positive relationships play a critical role in shaping the character and well-being of a community. Whether it is through promoting a sense of connection, fostering resilience and support, reducing conflicts and tensions, or any of the other many benefits of positive relationships, it is clear that these relationships can have a profound impact on the health and happiness of communities everywhere

THIRTY

Positive relationships can also have a profound impact on global connections. When people from different cultures, backgrounds, and beliefs come together in a positive and respectful way, it can help to build bridges and create understanding between different groups of people. This can lead to a more peaceful and harmonious world, as people learn to appreciate and celebrate their differences rather than seeing them as barriers.

In today's interconnected world, positive relationships are more important than ever. With the rise of social media and the internet, people are more connected than ever before. This means that the impact of positive relationships can be felt all over the world, as people from different countries come together to share ideas, support one another, and work towards common goals.

For example, positive relationships between countries can lead to better international cooperation on issues such as climate change, economic development, and human rights. When countries work together in a positive and respectful way, they are more likely to find solutions that are beneficial for everyone involved.

In addition, positive relationships between individuals from different countries can help to break down cultural barriers and increase understanding between different cultures. This can lead to a more tolerant and inclusive world, where people from all walks of life are able to coexist in peace and respect one another's differences.

Overall, the power of positive relationships in global connections cannot be overstated. By fostering positive relationships between individuals and countries, we can work towards a more connected, harmonious, and understanding world.

THIRTY-ONE

CONCLUSION: THE ENDLESS BENEFITS OF POSITIVE RELATIONSHIPS

In conclusion, positive relationships have countless benefits for individuals, communities, and the world at large. These relationships, whether they are romantic, familial, platonic, or professional, bring joy, fulfillment, and a sense of belonging to our lives. They improve our mental and physical health, enhance our career success, and contribute to our financial stability. Positive relationships also help us to overcome challenges and conflicts, practice self-care and set boundaries, and expand our perspectives through diversity and inclusiveness. Furthermore, investing in quality time, learning, and growth can only enhance the power of positive relationships.

Positive relationships can have a ripple effect, not only improving our personal lives but also impacting our relationships with others and our communities. They help build bridges and create a sense of belonging and connectedness in a world that can often feel divisive. The power of positive relationships extends globally, as we connect and collaborate with others from different backgrounds, cultures, and nations.

In short, the benefits of positive relationships are endless and essential for a fulfilling and happy life. By prioritizing and nurturing our relationships, we can reap the many rewards that come with positive connections.